stylish solutions

Clarkson Potter/Publishers
New York

stylish solutions

what you can do about a coffee table...
and answers to other decorating dilemmas

Elizabeth Gaynor and Kari Haavisto

**In memory of
Emanuel Gaynor**

Published by Clarkson N. Potter/Publishers, 201 East 50th Street, New York, New York 10022. Member of the Crown Publishing Group.

Random House, Inc. New York, Toronto, London, Sydney, Auckland
www.randomhouse.com

CLARKSON N. POTTER, POTTER, and colophon are trademarks of Clarkson N. Potter, Inc.

Printed in China
Designed by Bernard Scharf

Library of Congress Cataloging-in-Publication Data
Gaynor, Elizabeth.
   Stylish solutions / Elizabeth Gaynor and Kari Haavisto. — 1st ed.
   Includes index.
   1. Interior decoration—Handbooks, manuals, etc.   I. Haavisto, Kari.
   II. Title.
NK2115.G33   1998
747—dc21   98-15173
                                                   CIP
ISBN 0-517-70452-8

10   9   8   7   6   5   4   3   2   1

First Edition

The authors wish to give special thanks to Walter Anderson, Gayle Benderoff, Gemma Comas, Marja Fellman, Roy Finamore, Anne Gaynor, Deborah Geltman, Samuli Haavisto, Reneé Keller-Johnson, Barbara McMahon, Joyce Ravid, and all those who opened their doors.

Photograph pages 32–33 reprinted with permission of *Home* magazine.
Rooms on pages 24, 66, 75 (top), 90, 96, and 134 from the American Hospital of Paris 1995 French Designer Showhouse.

title page: Doug Turshen and Rochelle Udell use an old enamel-top kitchen table as a sideboard, occasionally pulling up a chair or two when they need extra seating. Their collection of antique fruit prints, picked up a couple at a time, eventually grew large enough to make major impact on the better part of the adjacent wall. Striped wallpaper helped to organize the prints and keeps them lined up.

contents

introduction

Successful design always solves problems—with

function, aesthetics, and a bit of serendipity.

The goal of this book is to present

these problems in succinct visual bites, in

targeted areas of rooms. Problems like where to

place the sofa, how to arrange things on

the coffee table, what to make of a bed.

There isn't one right answer. There are many,

not only because of the range in physical

variables and practical needs, but

because there is infinite variety in what is

attainable, acceptable, and fashionable in interiors

today. This is a book of alternatives, a

broad showcase of stylish solutions. Here are

smart, realizable proposals that could lure you into

a weekend makeover or spark a longer

project. This is a look at how to find and

put together the elements, and ways to rearrange

what you've got. It's not just about what

you include, but the empty space you

leave around it. We have photographed locations

that are scrupulously and wittily designed,

but—clearly—lived in. We tap the ideas

of designers, architects, stylists, art directors, and

others with a good eye. We talk about getting

results and about the need to create

something when it can't be found. Behind the

particulars of their designs are

fundamentals that make their methods universally

applicable and their solutions stylish:

Everyone comes with baggage, so working

out a plan involves creative reuse of things you own.

Having to recombine and resituate furnishings

changes their relationships and serves

as an incubator of new ideas. Being able to

visualize results isn't a given, even for professionals.

Often they mock up things with

stand-in furniture or cardboard forms,

to feel spatial changes before they implement

them or before making a major purchase.

Balance is basic; that's why it's

pleasing and has endured as a design ideal.

Master symmetry first, then test out departures
to sidestep the expected. Sometimes
people purchase a piece of furniture to fill a
specific space or need, but just as often they simply
buy what they can't resist, without knowing
exactly where it will fit in. Then they find a
way to make it work. Style isn't intrinsically pricey.
Humble finds in knowing hands become
unique fittings that hold their own next to
objects of fine pedigree. Finally, creators realize they
don't have to reinvent the wheel. They
recognize a great look when they see it and
have the courage to go with it. It's our hope that,
with this book as incentive, you will too.

coffee table

There's no historic precedent for what
we've come to think of as a coffee table. It's a
20th-century contrivance. The tea table in service
of a settle got lopped off around the knees,
metaphorically, to make it accessible from our
lower-slung sofas. This fact considerably frees up
contemporary interpretations of what qualifies
as a coffee table. Its relationship to adjacent
seating is paramount. As to materials, almost
anything goes, but the table's usefulness and the
guests' inclination to use it will be affected by
the choice. Coffee tables should hold a few
appealing curios of varying heights and textures
but always offer space to put something down.

It's possible to choose a coffee table for a formal living room that is both functional and refined. Victoria Hagan found one with a durable limestone surface and a modern take on a footed iron base. The designer disdains the crowded tabletop, preferring a bowl of fruit and cut flowers in a setting where minimal furnishings act as a serene foil for an art collection.

Donna Gorman envisioned a "big football-shaped surface" as her coffee table and had it made from a 1-inch slab of Australian lacewood, *opposite.* Modeled on the curves of the Eames table, this one is larger and lower, often filling in as a place to eat when pillows are scattered around for guests. The 8-foot-long oval hovers a mere 10 inches above the sisal rug on custom-made iron legs "so, at that size, it doesn't take over the room." Donna cut a piece of foam core to mock up the shape before finalizing its proportions. Glossy lacquer protects the exotic wood so guests feel at ease using it for food and drink.

floral designer Jennifer Houser considers a coffee table a necessary evil. "It's hard to find anything interesting, but people do need to put their drinks down," she concedes. This 19th-century folding picnic table is just unusual enough to have caught her eye at an antiques show, and it's sufficiently marred to encourage use in a living room that's the hub of a Greek Revival house. Doors on three sides prompted Jennifer to float the velvet-upholstered seating around the piece. For dinner parties, the table resumes its old role as a place to take dessert and coffee.

D BABY MAKES THREE

a coffee table's role is in part determined by the character of the seating elements it serves. Where a wood bench acts as secondary seating—and its uprightness doesn't invite lounging or even prolonged visits—the table's purpose becomes more tightly defined, the demands on its function more limited. A case in point: the quirky turn-of-the-century ostrich-leg specimen *above,* succinctly designated by designer Victoria Hagan as just enough space for a cup of tea. She left its brass finish as found, slightly tarnished, in congruence with the vintage feel of the setting. A lone orchid accentuates the table's verticality against the broad bench. A William Morris print covers the throw pillow.

kristiina Ratia demands a lot of a coffee table: that it be scaled to hold generous amounts of food, sturdy enough to put your feet on, and a magnet for conversation with guests. A believer in coercing furnishings to perform as she desires, she didn't hesitate to cut inches off the legs of this French Provincial cherry dining table, to bring it down to the right height for her sofas, *opposite.* A couple of carved, early-19th-century Finnish betrothal chairs pulled up close to its long, open side provide auxiliary seating when her family of six, plus friends, want to gather.

living low in a room with a view gains the space light by day and sparkle at night. William Diamond and Anthony Baratta established a low horizon in the spacious living room of an apartment in a sleek urban tower, prompted by the openness of the floor plan and the potential of the window walls for dramatic effect. The designers had banquettes built in to hug the ivory-carpeted floor. Their coffee table design shares the low center of gravity. They see it as a "folded plane," a 2-inch thickness of wood that simply "goes up, across, and down." When they couldn't find one on the market, they created it. The coffee table is the color of thick cream, lacquered so it's impervious to the moisture of a drink or a vase. A wicker basket keeps magazines at bay, relieving the tabletop of that duty.

artist Richard Giglio came up with a split-level solution to the coffee table dilemma, *left*. An old white games table, cut down from 30-inch height, manages the clutter, freeing up the delicate 1920s Moroccan table butted up against it. The brass piece shines amid fittings visually linked by metallic touches.

a slatted washtub stand found at a flea market became a coffee table in an all-white room relieved by naturals, *left*. Bleached and marred by years of drenchings, the wooden piece is intrinsically childproof. Stylist Tricia Foley likes to stack it with books; a snack is easily balanced on top.

the elliptical table of plywood and metal, made by Chris Lehrecke, was chosen by stylist Peter Frank to juxtapose with his Biedermeier sofa, *opposite*. On top, he favors a rotation of curios and always includes something tactile—like the set of mandrels, once used to shape spoons. He finds a tight knot of flowers in old silver more romantic than a big arrangement.

an attraction of opposites accounts for the
successful pairing of a 17th-century sailor's chest
from Finland with contemporary white leather
sofas. The dark wood and simple ironwork braces
of the trunk offer depth in a town house sitting
room where whites hold forth in upholstery, floor
tile, and walls. Two sofas in an L-layout balance
the weight of the chest. Disparate flower
containers are modern and traditional, useful and
decorative, representative of the duality of other
furnishings. The white lilacs and lilies of the valley
keep the look clean. Marja Berg, an art collector
and writer, had the vision to bring it together.

In a room designed by Sheryl Rock and Jorge Letelier, a gutsy steel coffee table sits on a fine 19th-century Persian carpet. "Opposites enhance" explains why they work too with a Louis XV stool. The designers had the table fabricated to frame a Roman floor fragment. A sculpture by Gloria Ries is centered on top; the mosaic antiquity requires little ornamentation. Centuries of use have proven the floor fragment's indestructibility, bequeathing it a literal put-your-feet-up appeal.

a small chest and a child's chair stand in for the conventional coffee table in a den oriented toward TV-watching and reading in Kristiina Ratia's home. More than a place to display objects, these are working elements that are also appealing antiques. The chest holds a throw and a supply of candles; a basket organizes strategic TV gadgetry. The chair keeps magazines neatly piled. The chest-chair combo offers a quick way to restore order to a much-used room at the end of a day.

The living room of Isabelle Stevenson, president of The American Theatre Wing, is a pastiche of art and mementos mingled with fine antiques. She found a Venetian stool in London and seized upon it as a genteel alternative to a coffee table amid a sofa and a suite of Louis XV chairs. She re-covered the stool in coral suede and had a thick slab of acrylic cut to lay on top, bringing it into the 20th century as an unexpected platform for contemporary sculpture as well as cocktails.

Her grandfather's round Empire table centers a mix of old and built-in furniture in designer Susan Ratcliff's sitting room, *opposite*. The space serves as dressing room and upstairs TV area too: clothing and equipment are stored in the cupboard and drawers. The tea table height is convenient for a sewing project or a snack over a book. The dark finish reads as a curvy silhouette in the white space.

It's there and not there—this just-big-enough glass table that floats between a chair and an Empire settee in a room by Victoria Hagan and her late partner, Simone Feldman, *right*. In small spaces like this one, scale and transparency are key to success. Pieces profiled like these against a neutral background "take on their own personality," according to Victoria. A flower-arranging frog that supports a fragrant stalk and two mushrooms provides just enough adornment.

a low white block of a table stretches the full length of the nubby cotton couch in the home of the late Armi Ratia, founder of Marimekko, *below.* Large gatherings and a love of informality dictated the table's generous size. Greens and flowers hug the surface, emphasizing its breadth. Rhododendron and vines clipped just outside the house are arranged in a shallow container set on a glass platter. Votive candles are interspersed with tendrils that trail across the table naturalistically, for atmospheric night-lighting.

rather than shout for attention, the extravagantly mixed elements in the small room, *opposite,* seem to thrive in harmony. Charles Riley, who admits the combination is "not quite explainable," took a jewel-box attitude, layering "gems on gems." He didn't design the ice-blue table for this room, but he liked the way it injected some freshness into a jumble of warm-toned patterns. The table has an aniline-dyed green wood base and a top and apron of bronze-framed, reverse-painted glass. The silk-screened crosshatch pattern is the work of artist Gail Leddy. Metallic accessories, including a footed brass dish with cabochon agates, and brilliant flowers up the sparkle.

In room decor, movement means options. A coffee table on casters slides away from a heavy couch for ease of cleaning or to open up traffic space for parties. This clear maple table fitted with metal tube legs was bought at Ikea, but its simple boxy construction lends itself to duplication by a cabinetmaker or a competent home carpenter. A dividend is its suspended shelf, hung via wraparound metal braces, a spot for magazines, newspapers, or jigsaw puzzles. The shelf slides to any convenient position, so the braces need felt liners affixed to them, to avoid scratching the wood. Among objects aboveboard are a flotilla of chunky candles on a tin tray and a flat of grass.

an acrylic bar cart wheels up to the banquette in Maggy Fellman's sitting room/studio. She chose it as much for its invisibility as for its practicality. In a room with a southern exposure, daylight floods right through the cart, accenting its contents. It serves a cushioned, built-in deck intended for relaxing, reading, and sleeping—a clear-the-mind area in a space envisioned as a modern garret for painting and desk work.

Mark McDonald maintains that simple architectonic things from most periods are compatible. Witness his own apartment, *above,* an amalgam of signature pieces bought not for a specific setting but because he responded to their design. Among them is a set of 1930s nested tables by Marcel Breuer that expand to coffee-table width and contract as needed. Favorite pieces rotate between here and McDonald's Gansevoort Gallery for classic modern furnishings, in New York City.

I biked by this funny table and pulled over," says Sara Vass, "and then hauled it home in a cab." The silver reverse-painted glass top with blue stenciling, *right,* sits on a gold-rubbed wood base of indeterminate breed. At first glance, the setup looks conventional. In fact, the medley of pale color and pattern, from unmatched sofa fabrics to beaded pillow to Towle pot, is as eccentric as the table's provenance.

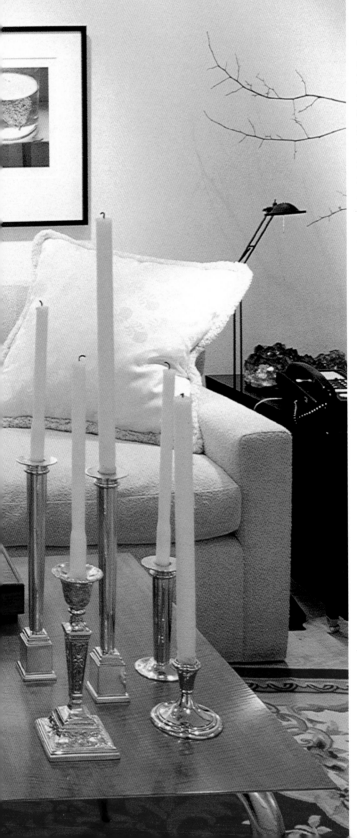

designer Bruce Bierman is a master at using refined materials in understated contemporary ways. He concocted this wafer-thin coffee table by marrying a piece of anigre wood with a set of curvy steel legs that he appropriated from a Philippe Starck chair—a modern take on Queen Anne style. He had the wood beveled on the underside (it's 1½ inches thick, thinner toward the edges), then stained it and gave it a satin urethane finish. Accessories are also of wood and metal. Gauze gives a fashionable wrap to a flat of orchids. A handsome lacquer box camouflages TV remote controls. The table stands before a big, cushy sofa, 9 feet by 39 inches, covered in nubby cream silk, where Bruce goes horizontal after long days on the run with clients. The alley between table and couch is minimal. "Don't think of it as a thoroughfare," he advises. "You should be able to reach over and easily put something down." Photos by Jeannette Montgomery Barron are hung low, in a sight line with the orchids and candlesticks, at a level geared to seating height.

a pair of sofas faces off with a pair of slim coffee tables in a room where people are drawn to walk right through the middle, toward the patio and an ocean view. The inch-thick glass that tops the X-base steel tables zaps a streak of electric blue across a neutral environment of ribbed linen carpet and cotton-covered sofa with leather trim in a vintage modern house. Accessories are staged to be seen in layers across two tablescapes. The interior, sofa, and table design are by Daniel Barsanti and Patricia Healing.

- **Have a trough of** wood made with 5-inch sides and 12-inch legs. Paint it a neutral tone and display collections inside. Lay a piece of glass over it as a coffee-table surface.

- **Attach casters to** the legs of a coffee table used in front of a sleep sofa so it can be moved away easily when the bed is rolled out.

- **Buy an ottoman** instead of a coffee table and put your feet up without guilt. Set a large wicker or lacquer tray on top to adapt it to table use, as needed.

- **Hang a pair of** minimalist halogen lamps low over a coffee table to spotlight curios or a cluster of flowers.

- **Construct** matching triangular solids, about 20 inches high, with different laminated or painted finishes to use as paired coffee tables. Position them with their long sides parallel but not touching, so they are seen as distinct forms.

- **Stack several** large, flat cushions under a coffee table to be pulled out for extra seating or informal, low-level dining.

- **Center a round** coffee table among four club or wing chairs and do without a sofa.

- **Stack books on** a coffee table and use them as little pedestals to vary the heights of the objects you display.

- **Bring a rusted** metal garden table indoors and plant it in front of a sofa, for a rough-against-smooth look. Sand it lightly and finish it with flat urethane.

- **Choose a stocky** wood, metal, or masonry coffee table rather than a delicate specimen so friends can perch on it when you entertain.

- **Rethink your** coffee-table display if you're the parent of a toddler. Appeal to your inner child with a still life of graphic wooden toys, puzzles, and play figures.

sideboard/cupboard

Console, buffet, hutch, chest-on-chest, sideboard,

cupboard—these are pieces made for service.

In our perception of a room, they usually play

second fiddle to splashier furnishings, like a

couch, a bed, or a table dressed for dinner.

We depend on these humbler pieces to perform

behind the scenes. Most have storage as their

raison d'être, but some are also called upon

to make an entrance to a room unforgettable, some

to provide a surface to drop things on in

passing, others to wait patiently until they're

pressed into service for a particular occasion.

Whether lowly or grand of purpose, all

have the capacity to show off a bit too.

Cramming a glass-fronted cupboard full of textiles provides equal rations of storage and colorful rummage-sale eye appeal, *left.* Designer Charles Riley's collected remnants will find use later in pieced upholstery or as pillow covers. In the meantime, stashing his inventory of old and new yard goods here, with a couple of dolls sandwiched in, suits this 1880s pine Italian store fixture with turned columns. A pair of flame-shaped finials and a jug on top draw the eye up to the ceiling's decorative texturing.

doug Turshen found the built-in cupboard, *opposite,* painted all white in all white surroundings, to be so self-effacing it begged some finishing touch to distinguish it. Rather than add an ornamental cornice, he stirred interest by topping if off with a jumble of objects united only by their scale and whiteness. Hanging the graphic LUNCH sign behind the no-color grouping seems to pull it into focus.

Skirt an old kitchen table with linen and lay a thin slab of honed slate on top, and what do you get? A sideboard immaculately dressed for the dining room, *opposite*. The ominously sharp stone edges and corners were rounded to soften them. The skirt with inverted pleats is stiff enough to hang well; oversize serving pieces hide underneath. Interior designer Victoria Hagan counteracts the symmetry of the topiaries on top with unmatched side chairs and uncontained fruit.

a shortage of wall space didn't deter design editor Doug Turshen from finding a spot in his dining room for a narrow table, originally bought for a foyer, that serves here as a sideboard. The unorthodox treatment works because the tabletop lines up with the windowsills and its length is visually balanced by the series of framed toiles de Jouy fabric remnants hung vertically between the windows. The two-tiered table houses a rotation of offbeat collections, including a bowl of wax fruit, a faux bois lamp, and 1950s mugs.

This unusual collection of Venetian glass balls found a permanent home on Brian McCarthy's Austrian Biedermeier secretary. The interior designer bought the contemporary pieces, blown in the 18th-century style and always sold in groups of seven for good luck, along with their turned-wood stands, in Lyon, France. Brian works for a varied "skyline" in a room, juxtaposing heights and standing things on other things. The cherry wood secretary's curvaceous superstructure, which incorporates a hidden drawer, beckons as an obvious display platform. But the vivid crystal ball–like spheres staged at different heights offer surprise atop the period piece.

i bought it as junk," says fashion designer Joan Vass of her old New Mexican pie safe. Now it houses her seemingly infinite assortment of small-scale found objects, which includes sea fans, sand dollars, coral, and shells picked up in her travels to Morocco, Anguilla, and Italy, tiny porcelain mermaid dolls, and stones spotted along Manhattan's FDR Drive. She interprets her need to amass and display as an attempt to bring order to her life. The roughness of the peeling, bruised cupboard provides a weathered setting for her mostly natural finds. "I dust everything inside once a year," she says.

This 1830s pewter cupboard made in Massachusetts holds antique American spongeware. Collectors and dealers Sanford and Patricia Lynch Smith like having their service pieces on view and at arm's length. The cupboard dominates one wall of the kitchen, giving an unfitted-kitchen character to an area with conventional storage, appliances, and a butcher-block island. The open shelves hold pottery that is used at table plus a few rarities reserved for display. Linens, glasses, and such are kept behind the doors below. A built-in closet (used as a stash for cleaning gear) in the adjacent dining area echoes the hutch in scale. The lineup of American stoneware jugs across the tops of both cupboards creates a mirror effect and carries the eye right past a load-bearing half wall, the only indication that the kitchen is an addition at the rear of the town house.

When budget is an issue, a skirted pressed-wood table can do dining room buffet service rather gracefully, *right*. Interior designer Michael Foster set this one up in the Scandinavian idiom, elaborating on Ikea's Gustavian furnishings. A pair of footed wire bowls and a cake stand provide balance, 18th-century style.

Architect James Biber designed the low cabinet, *below*, to give a storage function to an alcove off a living room. He specified anigre and beech woods with their grains turned in opposite directions to contrast the door fronts. The drawer on top, a structural component, serves as stage for vintage cocktail shakers.

In an apartment with limited space—is there any other kind?—every piece of furniture has to justify its existence. Writer and stylist Carole Manchester's 19th-century mahogany English chest-on-chest, *opposite*, is elegant but works hard. She's able to pack a load of linens and out-of-season clothing into its deep drawers, and even presses into service the cavity on top. Dried hydrangeas and roses tidily camouflage the candles and wrapping-paper rolls that just fit into the shallow space behind the classic cornice.

an empty space can foster a collection. Because the 19th-century English chinoiserie cabinet here stands only 5½ feet tall, it needed a cap. So says interior designer Charles Riley, who owned the large blue-and-white delft urn, for starters. He began to collect with an eye to how pieces would work together and continued until the surface was filled. Then he climbed the wall with three plates. The heavily distressed (read shabby chic) armoire and flawless assemblage of delftware are the more appealing for their contrast.

a typical Finnish farm cupboard, *left,* tucks into a kitchen corner between a bank of cabinets, a window, and a high shelf, as conceived by interior designer Kristiina Ratia. The cupboard's bug-in-a-rug fit is satisfyingly orderly, as are the filled-to-brimming shelves. Her service plates were too large to fit in, so she removed the upper doors. More china sits on built-ins, scales a wall, and perches on top of the cupboard, filling in the blanks.

accessories above, on, and below a leggy 19th-century Philippine table bulk it up to qualify as focal point in an entry hall, *opposite.* Interior designer Geertruda van Vliet anchored the table under a primitive portrait of her two daughters, painted by Dutch artist Anne-Marie Cartier. The painting's symmetry—executed so it can be cut and reframed as individual portraits later—dictates the balanced layout of accessories. A pair of 1920s bronze lamps casts a glow on iron ornaments and lidded containers. Flowers are cut short to keep the art visible.

hotelier and restaurateur Karl-Jan Granqvist let his banged-about Swedish country cupboard speak for itself. He was taken by its worn charm and so let it dictate the look of the surrounding walls, mottling them with a similar blue and a complementary ocher. A pair of Gustavian chairs keep the cupboard company in the dining room of his manor house. A dried nosegay adds a spot of faded color in keeping with the unpretentious piece.

the diminutive pine cupboard, *left,* feels more substantial when an old railroad clock is moored above it in the dining room of architects Carol Nelson and Harry de Polo. The 5-foot-tall Dutch chest has an accessible top, so objects both useful and whimsical find a place there: oil lamps and candlesticks, pieces of English and American silver, and a Japanese puppet head under a bell jar.

live large," designer Lynn Peterson advises her young clients. She chose the unusually long Directoire fruitwood buffet, *below,* for this dining room so that should the owners move to a bigger house, they need not trade up in scale. She emphasizes its horizontality in a series of framed renderings hung above and in accoutrements that run the length of the piece.

high contrast plays up the inside-outside appeal of this English pine cabinet, *opposite.* Designer Kristiina Ratia stained the wood dark and had the interior upholstered with an inky-blue-on-white toile de Jouy. This handsome solution makes an unexceptional cabinet look special and gives a background to transparent glassware. Upholstering adds some puff and cushions the glass. Crockery from the south of France crowns the whole with a bit of earthiness.

a 14-foot cabinet with a veneer of pearwood divides the open living/dining area in designer Donna Gorman's house. The cabinet straddles the floor surfaces, standing on large squares of matte white tile on the stepped-up dining side and buoyed up by industrial steel legs above a wood floor on the seating side. The long, low stretch of cabinet mimics the proportion of the dining table in a spacious room designed for entertaining. It encloses a TV, hi-fi equipment, and speakers on one side; liquor, linens, and serving pieces on the other. Reveals visually break its length, and wooden knobs punctuate the door fronts.

the fine lines of an iron console table and chair appear more linear against oak paneling that was stripped, lightly glazed, and waxed. In the dining room of a 19th-century town house, interior designer Victoria Hagan reversed the usual formula of dark paneling/light walls and had the walls glazed and waxed cerulean blue to give them a deep, dull patina. She replaced the table's original ivory travertine surface with blue slate so it looks all of a piece and accessorized it with a high-low lineup of Wedgwood basalt ware and laboratory beakers. A framed photograph reiterates the chiaroscuro of the objects and flowers.

Richard Lee's armoire stands near enough to a window so that orchids and anemone plants can be clustered on top, *left*. A painting on a stand and a pair of porcelain urns mix it up with cachepots and clay pots. Tones of amber, caramel, and custard relate to the neo-Gothic armoire's warm wood. The designer pleated green silk and stapled it to foam core boards, which he attached with L-hooks to the inside frames of the glass doors, so he could use the piece to conceal stereo equipment and CDs.

There's a simple clarity about this combination of elements, *opposite*. Refinishing an old apothecary cabinet to a high shine gave it new life as a sideboard in designer Don Black's apartment. You'd be hard put to guess that it's also an excellent organizer of hardware, tools, and string. A portrait of an Irish patriot hangs just a few inches above the cabinet, lending weight to the piece. A Chinese exportware platter and teapot reinforce the strong simplicity. Carved wood swan brackets pick up the gilding of the picture frame and extend the impact of the small cabinet in a traditional living room.

A series of reflector sconces hung low over a cupboard set the stage for Arts and Crafts pottery, *right*. Designer and artist Judyth van Amringe loves to embellish: she outlined the lighting elements whimsically and stenciled a few lines of poetry on the wall in lieu of hanging art. The dull green vases are handsome on their own, but fresh flowers can be contained in any number of them at will.

leaving a surface bare can call as much attention to it as filling it. This graceful George III étagère is used in a deliberately spare way in a poetically spare room decorated by Carlos Aparicio. He wanted the quiet antique to give definition to a corner between the hearth and a side wall. It's a niche that works for setting up hors d'oeuvre and cocktails. Upholstery tacks delineate panels of natural linen stretched over the wall and provide tailored backup for the étagère's crisp lines. A pool of light glows against a painting of a moonless night sky; crystal and silver objects glimmer underneath.

- **Stand a large** cupboard in a front or back hall and reconfigure the inside to function as a mini-mudroom. Install hooks and cubbyholes for gear; stow boots and umbrellas below.

- **Get a carpenter** to build a cupboard using a couple of old salvaged doors for the front. Stain or paint the cabinet in tones similar to those of the doors.

- **Crown an** armoire with dried bunches of flowers laid closely side-by-side, so they form a hedge of color across the top.

- **Line a basket** with an old worn sweater and set it on top of a cupboard for your cat's naps.

- **Hang a vertical** row of framed botanical prints, old maps, or silhouettes on either side of an armoire, from its top to the baseboard.

- **Position a table** and chair between a pair of matching cupboards (fitted with shelves to hold supplies) to turn one wall of a room into a home office.

- **Sew a long run-** ner for a dining room sideboard. Make it a few inches narrower than the surface and 10 to 12 inches longer so there's a drop on either end. Tack a tassel on each corner to add weight and a flourish.

- **Hang a broad** plate rack directly over a buffet to get the two pieces to do the work of a hutch. Attach hooks to the bottom for a row of teacups.

- **Use a sideboard** surface to display handsome, oversize pieces like soup tureens, a tea service, or decanters instead of storing them away.

- **Load a buffet** with fruits and vegetables in containers for decorative color—an alternative to cut flowers.

- **Use a buffet in** the living room to house the TV, VCR, and videotapes behind cabinet doors. Stack magazines across the top.

sofa

A sofa can be used for sitting, slouching,

snoozing, snacking, TV-watching, reading, or

perching at parties. A sofa can encourage

you to linger or imply the suitability of a short

visit. It may be the most important piece of

furniture in the living room, although its use is not

confined to that space. Wherever it stands, its

scale should reflect that of the room, and its

upholstery must complement nearby furnishings.

Pattern, color, and trim are infinitely variable.

Well-loved couches can live many lives with

a change of wardrobe as they become worn.

They can be reupholstered, slipcovered,

or layered with pillows, throws, and textiles.

the one-sofa rule is worth abandoning when space permits. Why not a whole fleet of them with related upholstery, some with backs and arms, some without? Color play is prominent in this all-of-a-kind seating group designed by James Biber for Dorothy and Jerome Kretchmer's home. He took inspiration from the 1920s work of Jean-Michel Frank and adapted it to the needs of a couple who love to entertain but also want to stretch out and read here in the evening. A living room with two three-seater sofas and an assortment of ottomans accommodates reading in a multitude of poses, and parties where guests can pivot for conversation. The high ottoman (far left) suits the long-legged who don't relish sinking into a low seat and the social birds who enjoy just perching and chattering at sofa-arm height. The upholstery is tight enough to balance a plate of food.

gathering fittings from different periods creates a timeless look and, according to designer Victoria Hagan, "makes people think a little." She and her late partner, Simone Feldman, pulled together a velvet-covered Italian gilt settee, a classic Bertoia wire chair, an end table custom-made as a stereo cube, and a white Bristol lamp, *below*. It's the punch of antique with modern, hand-carved with man-made, that causes notice.

If a living room is also an entry and a dining area, as in so many apartments, its design needs allure plus practicality. Charles Riley created a seating area that hugs a wall, *opposite*, giving it presence by centering it beneath a 19th-century carved mirror and a ring of medallions discovered in junk stores and antique shops. Another fanciful find was the majolica pedestal (a onetime jardiniere base) for which he had artist Gail Leddy faux-paint a butcher-block top to resemble a polychrome marble specimen piece. The table's wheel of color invites unmatched upholstery of any hue.

When the fabric on an upholstered piece wears thin, it's an opportunity to rethink the concept, not just the color. Carlos Mota took a Lawson sofa from straight to hip with contrasting fabric. He had the frame re-covered in black, the seat and back cushions in a graphic stripe, throw pillows in unmatched solids. The black is strong and fashionable, made bolder by an old classroom blackboard hung nearby that serves both as a surface for scribbling phone messages and as a blank slate for improvised art. A pair of cubes do the work of a coffee table.

designer Christopher Coleman fought tight space with overscale appointments in an impossibly small room allotted him in a decorator showhouse, *right*. A 66-inch-long daybed, with a 15-inch-thick bolster and a 30-inch-square pillow, nestles in a cocoon of curtaining on a window wall. Broad brown and cream stripes tie sofa to drapes to floor. A tiny table exaggerates the play on proportion.

Susan Ratcliff demonstrates that you don't have to push the couch right up against a wall, *below*. She turned her multilayered sofa at an angle (the rug follows) to take the boxiness out of a predictably rectangular room. The move yields a free corner for a container of branches.

fashion designer Joan Vass makes a career of color, texture, pattern, and line. A similar aesthetic carries over at home, but here it is tempered by loyalty to past possessions, family pass-alongs, the handwork of her children—stuff that is resistant to the changing winds of fashion. Her couches are cozy collages of overlaid textiles. A 1960s striped sleep sofa from Knoll, *left,* idiosyncratically welcomes a 19th-century paisley shawl and a medley of pillows: a few of needlepoint, a couple hooked (scraps came from her clothing line), and a matched pair of naively appliquéd felt ones that had been her mother's.

for much of my life I lived with no rugs on the floor, only on the furniture," Joan says. "I read about the Cone sisters in Baltimore, who used rugs like that." A kilim drapes one half of a sectional sofa by Paul McCobb, *right.* A couple of woven stripes, *above right,* are unaffectedly draped over the back and seat of the other half. The two single-armed units face each other across another kilim whose warm rosy tones relate to both.

a cut-velvet double camelback sofa skirted with deep fringe is cradled by a pair of bookcases in Brian McCarthy's library. He had the freestanding bookcases made and set them on an axis with the fireplace across the room. The niche thus formed creates a shadow box for the sofa and a frame for all fittings in its orbit. The wall behind, glazed a paper-bag tan, is a gutsy neutral foil. The painting is by Rubincamp, a 1930s American Expressionist. Brian's brand of tradition with bravado combines reproduction with antique, bold with delicate, emptiness with calculated clutter.

Carol Nelson cut a corner with an old love seat that was left in the 250-year-old farmhouse she bought. Too small to stand on its own along a wall in the front parlor, its curved back allows it to snuggle into this spot. A serviceable piece but not exactly a prize, it was slipcovered in sage green cotton to fade into the walls. Accompanying it with furnishings of some historical merit— a 19th-century ladies' writing table, rocker, smoke-painted trunk (candle soot was rubbed over the painted surface), and paisley shawl—is a way of helping to aggrandize its value.

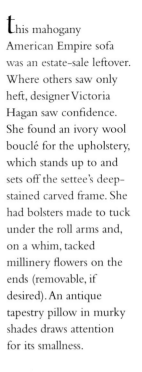

This mahogany American Empire sofa was an estate-sale leftover. Where others saw only heft, designer Victoria Hagan saw confidence. She found an ivory wool bouclé for the upholstery, which stands up to and sets off the settee's deep-stained carved frame. She had bolsters made to tuck under the roll arms and, on a whim, tacked millinery flowers on the ends (removable, if desired). An antique tapestry pillow in murky shades draws attention for its smallness.

Size was a factor in choosing this reproduction Biedermeier sofa for a living room where half of the space goes to seating, half to dining and desk work, *above*. Peter Frank got a good price on a display piece and re-covered it in sage velvet. He broods over the interaction of shape and proportion among furnishings as he shops, not over their period and style. A trio of tables are contemporary, Art Deco, and formally skirted in taffeta. Lamps and chairs are equally dissimilar. "My liking these things was the unifying element," he concludes. A warm neutral palette also connects them in a room that's bathed in cool northern light.

Kenneth Fishman found an outlandish cast-iron Spanish sleigh bed in an antique store and, with the help of designer Charles Riley, turned it into a sofa, *opposite*. Its width was cut down from double to twin size, leaving generous depth for seating. Pillows not only fill it out but fill it up, as woven-fabric and needlepoint remnants are found for the limitless pattern-on-patterning. "It's a throw-yourself-into-it-and-stay kind of sofa," Charles explains.

textile designer Anki Spets sees the organic gray-and-white linen print by Josef Frank—used on her sofa—as neutral ground, *below*. Afflicted with the designer's craving for change, she rotates the toss pillows (her prints) regularly, pretty much ignoring dicta about complementary pattern and color. "My kind of color is intense but not warm. If I stay in this range, it works," she explains. Nested tables echo organic curves elsewhere.

discipline prevents an unusual assortment of materials, styles, and colors from getting out of hand in a sitting room designed by Betsy Train, *opposite*. Her horse-country client begged her to stray from the purely vernacular and decorate with some opulence. She did it by revving up the typical country colors of the barn-board walls and ceiling—in a house by architect John Milner—and using them as a backdrop for a Louis XVI settee, French reproduction crystal sconces, and modern graphics. A footstool and down-filled pillows make the settee more sittable.

floating a daybed in front of a window and calling it a sofa has some advantages: puffy pillows, meant to be pummeled and pushed around, give personalized back support against the sill or at the ends. Daylight is a lure for the reader or mender. The view is a catalyst for daydreaming, a satisfying pastime, often overlooked in the been-there done-that era. Designer Christopher Coleman had the daybed frame covered in checks, the mattress in natural cotton. A cuddly Beacon blanket laid across it visually cuts the expanse of mattress and extends an invitation to stretch out. He let the inherent balance of the architecture dictate the symmetry of the layout. Salvaged radiator covers were lacquered black for end tables. Gilt-framed Hudson River School oils occupy the space on either side of the windows.

there are two ways to go with a period-style sofa: honor its history and use age-appropriate color and pattern—or do an about-face, as designer Richard Lee did with his Louis XVI reproduction settee. He gave it attitude with strident taxicab-yellow leather upholstery in contrast to the antiqued gray frame. The setting is also of the present—a bare floor, a few hooked scatter rugs, and one of his own oil still lifes relaxing against the wall, with a potted orchid reiterating the art.

- **Have a sofa** made in sections to get the grand scale you covet, but simplify the moving-in process by having the piece assembled in your living room.
- **Collect old** unmatched needlepoint pillows to set against a natural canvas–covered sofa.
- **Lay a long** striped rag runner (a Scandinavian staple) across the seat of a solid-color sofa.
- **Turn a sofa on** an angle in a corner and stand a folding screen behind it.
- **Slipcover your** bright throw pillows in solid black or white organdy to give them a filmy, color-seen-through-color allure.
- **Fill the wall** directly above a couch with a double row of framed graphics, hung closely side by side.
- **Make up floppy** toss pillows and lay one in each sofa corner and another over the corner back, freeing up seating space.
- **Wrap worn** upholstery with a patchwork quilt or Marseilles bedspread of about the same width as the sofa. Start from the back and wrap down over the back and the seat cushions, tucking it in slightly to anchor it where the back meets the deck.
- **Put a futon to** work in the daytime as a couch. Construct a blocky base of wood, paint it black, and position it against a wall. Make up four overscale squares stenciled with large gold leaves for use as back cushions. Stand them side by side in a double row.
- **Tuft, channel-** quilt, pipe, fringe, or add trim to the back and seat cushions to change the look of a sofa instead of replacing it.
- **Think dropcloth** as you make a muslin slipcover. Sew up a boxy form that hangs loosely over the sofa to relax it and make it appear more volumetric.

bookcase

Bookshelves are like money: most of us never have enough. The storage space they provide is rapidly claimed but seldom relinquished. People are loath to give away books (even those they infrequently read) the way they do clothes or other old possessions. A bookcase can span a whole wall, framing windows and doors, or be cleverly rigged to make use of leftover space. In some of the nicest, books share space with beautiful objects, photographs, or art. Of all furnishings, bookshelves are among the easiest to build, so the range in their sophistication and intrinsic value is great. For those who love to read, books add warmth and familiarity to any room in the house.

Sometimes a bookcase isn't. This bench of clear birch plywood was conceived by Donna Gorman to fill a vacant niche in her bedroom, not really as a seating element but as a spot to drop clothes or leave shopping bags. It evolved into a place to pile oversize books and magazines; clothing can still be tossed over the stacks. For its form, she looked to the Scandinavian-style wooden daybeds made in the 18th and 19th centuries—the kind that convert from bench to a pair of twin beds via a trundle drawer. Her deliberately flat, simplified interpretation is not meant for sleeping, but for aesthetics—a bench drawn for line, not comfort. Books laid here are new acquisitions or of current interest; they move on to a conventional bookcase as they lose their edge. Some spill over onto the side table or floor. A raffia pillow and an occasional artwork add texture.

Kristiina Ratia lined one wall of her long, rectangular living room with books, foreshortening the space and creating a reading area for her family of six. Her design bridges a gap between two doorways but also between the two decorating styles in which she works—modern and traditional. The bookcase is essentially a clean white three-bay arrangement, but it is ever so lightly embellished with vertical fluting. Its height was determined by the adjacent openings. The marble-topped French bistro table that stands in front designates this as a place to stop and peruse; a hanging lamp throws light on the subject at hand. An English library ladder and chair encourage use. The top of the bookcase showcases the designer's collection of miniature chairs.

Photographer Anita Calero claims to lay down her books so they don't warp. The stacks also put to use an awkward space in the narrow entry of her apartment, *left*. A bench that once served as a place to sit and remove shoes or put them on, according to custom in her native Colombia, was commandeered for book storage when other walls filled. As the piles grew, she saw added potential—to display art, shapely stones, a string of beads.

Cookbooks often go looking for a good home. Brian McCarthy commingles them with china and packaged food in his kitchen corner, *below*. They rest on a wood radiator cover and climb the walls, contained by the bracket shelves he devised for this purpose.

a bookcase can also be a showcase—when objects are purposely integrated to break up the heavy look of wall-to-wall volumes, or sometimes as a stopgap measure until new books beg housing. Designer Marc Donnenfeld liked the boniness of this slim unit designed by Pascale Mourgue, *opposite,* and felt no compulsion to pack it with books. He gave books and art equal shares of shelf space, treating each as worthy of attention.

a master of presentation, owing to a career in furniture buying and retailing, Don Black pulled off a rather convincing antiquated English library look in the altogether ordinary spare bedroom of his apartment. Having concluded that the space would best be utilized as a library/guest room, he performed his alchemy by means of a tufted leather-look sofa bed (now peeling) and custom-made bookcases. No elaborate fabrication fillips required—just floor-to-ceiling shelf units constructed in sections so they can be shifted or moved out. The sides are perforated and the shelves hung on spacers so they can be repositioned. Imaginative styling facilitates the desired effect: portraits and busts integrated into the bookcases, library and picture lights that glow on the honey-toned wood, a coffee table made from an Irish regiment drum topped off with a round of black glass and an old globe.

a narrow slice of wall between two doors furnished just enough space for the restaurant-supply tray cart that stylist Carlos Mota transformed into a bookcase, *left*. He had glass shelves cut to size and spaced them far enough apart to accommodate his art and architecture books. The aluminum carriage can be wheeled into the bedroom when he wants more standing room for parties.

Wall brackets of brushed aluminum in Peter Frank's bedroom are a stylist's smooth update on metal standards, *below*. Supports slide along a track and are held in place with aluminum pins. U-shaped shelves are 8 inches by 4 feet, a span that won't buckle under the weight of books. The shelves are neatly beveled at the corners, exploiting the birch plywood to decorative effect.

designer Brian McCarthy chose a low bookcase instead of an end table in his den, *opposite*. The French Empire walnut sleigh bed and fabric-covered walls are the dominant elements. The raw wrought-iron bookcase with wood shelves is decidedly recessive, but it fits the snug space, offering more than just a surface to hold a drink. Its iron frame was lightly sanded and rubbed with oil to freeze-frame the rusted surface. A portrait of Brian's great-grandfather is propped up on the top shelf, magnifying the intended contrast of fancy versus plain, grand versus meager.

$m$aggy and Klaus Fellman saw the potential in a staircase wall when their architect, Esko Lehismaa, presented them with plans for the addition that doubled the size of their house. The cutoff wall they proposed netted them an expanse of bookshelves that is the envy of anyone addicted to reading abed. The shelves are of clear pine, like the walls and ceiling, and are likewise treated to a bath of titanium white, to avert yellowing, and sealed with satin varnish. The cutoff portion allows daylight to wash into the stairwell and serves as a handrail.

Salvaged drugstore fittings were recycled into a bookcase along one wall in fashion designer Joan Vass's loft. By removing one section of shelves, she jiggered them to fit around a doorway. An old door, whose zigzag design holds its own against the relief work of the cornice and pilasters, was hung in the bedroom entrance. A length of Liberty of London fabric was folded and affixed to a roller to create a shade for privacy. Books abound, overflowing onto the counters, conjuring up a comfortable reading-room ambience.

In anticipation of the bookcase wall he envisioned for one side of his living room, designer Randy Ridliss began to stack books there, by a mahogany Georgian architect's table. Taken by the look, he abandoned the idea of shelves altogether. He's neat enough by nature to make the arrangement work and distinctly symmetrical in design attitude, in keeping with the 18th-century style he admires. The baskets in the foreground give substance to the stacks as a treatment, and objects poised among the piles lend decorating credence to the idea. Books are placed strategically to leave kneehole room under the table.

In a unit configured for books, stereo equipment, and a cookie jar collection, *below,* shelves frame other shelves around an opening. Architect James Biber specified hollow plywood construction to bulk up the dimensions of the wall-hung grid. A pair of deep cabinets—scaled to house record albums and discs—appear, plinthlike, to support the shelving.

Causing the eye to see things past other things enriches the field of vision. For a living room corner, Randy Ridliss contrived an upright little bookcase to hold his architecture and design books, and positioned it squarely between the hearth and a window, *opposite.* Although he allowed for clearance to move around and pluck down a reference, he exaggerated the layering of objects above, on, and in front of the piece. The bookcase was fabricated from stock lumber boards and trim, following his drawing, based on 18th-century examples. The built-up cornice is hollow, permitting the wire for an art lamp that highlights a set of Italian intaglios to pass through to the wall behind the case.

a bank of shelves utilizes space under a row of windows for book storage, *left*. The blond wood elements were designed by Peter Superti for Mark McDonald. Sections stack; some are fronted with sliding wood doors, others with doors of perforated metal, creating variation in the components. Venetian blinds are of a compatible light wood for continuity.

even those with carefully thought out rooms may stoop to floor level when coming up with creative solutions to the problem of what to do with more books. Brian McCarthy, whose ferreting-out of decorative objects for clients often turns up irresistible prizes for himself, determined that the floor was the best temporary (or permanent) spot for some of each. He used piles of art books as columns to support a pair of English Towle lanterns, and framed a small 19th-century Chinese lacquer cabinet with them—filling space beneath a gilded mirror in his library/dining room, *opposite*.

"Our bookcase is like a high chair-rail," says Doug Turshen. Indeed, it cuts the height of the room and yields a surface where art and collections can be paraded. He and his wife, Rochelle Udell, took their design cues from the style of the trimwork elsewhere in their 1830 house. This writing and reading room is meant to feel warm and familial, a place to lessen the drudgery of take-home work for the couple, who are both magazine editors. The volumes provide a colorful tactile backdrop to a French fruitwood table that butts up against them. Doug's grandmother's old upholstered chair and a needlepoint footstool cozy up. Books are within reach of all family members.

- **Use oak stair** treads purchased from a lumberyard to build shallow bookshelves for paperbacks.
- **Designate a** portion of a bookcase for decorative objects or a painting. Remove one shelf and install a mini-spotlight to light this section.
- **Commission a** cabinetmaker to construct an open-grid bookcase and use it as a freestanding room divider.
- **Use odd wall** space for bookshelves. Configure them to wrap around adjacent furniture or zigzag past an architectural element.
- **Break down the** bookcase-as-rectangle barrier. Design one in the form of a pyramid or circle.
- **Run bookshelves** up the wall behind a bed, incorporating the headboard into the plan.
- **Build two or** three tall, slim bookcases, hinge them together, and freestand them like a folding screen.
- **Stand a pair of** urns or vases on the front corners of a tall bookcase as instant "finials."
- **Frame a door or** windows with bookshelves painted a contrasting color, giving depth to the openings.
- **Build out a wall** with Sheetrock to hide heating elements or pipes, then cut in a bookcase. Finish all sides with wallboard, install high-hat lamps in the soffit, and span the niche with glass shelves. Alternate decorative objects and books.
- **Use upholstery** tacks to call out the lines of an otherwise ordinary bookcase. Evenly space them along the fronts of shelves and vertical supports.
- **Hang a library-**green roller shade across the top of a bookcase filled with old volumes or rare books, so it can be rolled down, as needed, to prevent damage from direct sunlight.

mantel

A fireplace gives presence to a room

and prominence to a wall. If you have one,

you can't ignore it, but that doesn't mean

all adjacent furniture must be oriented in its

direction. If you don't have one, you can

bring in a mantel, old or new, just to

give a room a bit of architecture. A

chimneypiece can be highly ornamental and

require very little embellishment, or be very

plain. It provides a natural, although expected,

place to hang a large mirror or painting.

A mantel is really a shelf of sorts, as welcoming

to found objects of almost any height, artfully

arranged, as to valuable antiques.

The fireplace wall, *above,* becomes a studied composition in the hands of architects Carol Nelson and Harry de Polo. The door and the built-in cupboards, original to the 1700s farmhouse, interact with the mantel, making the wall a canvas of sorts. A banister-back chair, embroidered pillow, English coal scuttle, and painting command primary attention. Items on the mantel are seen as tiny treasures within the whole.

there's not just one white," reports Tricia Foley, stylist and author of *The Natural Home.* "There's linen, cream, ivory, fog, chalk, china." A longtime crusader for the space-enlarging, anything-goes properties of the white look, she demonstrates the effect, *left.* Tricia marches a line of objects across her 1845 mantel, varying them in tone and texture, and interspersing blush roses and the odd wicker bottle. In this no-contrast scheme, the carved vintage mantel is given the spotlight. The white shapes play supporting roles.

a small, undistinguished brick fireplace required handling to live up to the sleek renovation of Donna Gorman's house by architects Mojgan and Gisue Hariri. Their architectonic solution gave the whole wall importance as a streamlined, self-contained unit. A wash of gray stucco camouflages the old brick. A 6-inch-deep honed-slate mantel inscribes a narrow stripe across the wall that's reiterated by the raised slate hearth. Pottery is all of a kind and widely spaced, stretching the field of focus.

brushed steel is the material of choice for the catchy little box suspended from one end of the slate mantel. A contrivance intended by the architects to keep matches at hand, the sculptural cube found additional use as a light box for votive candles. They can be used to warm the appearance of the gray masonry even when the fireplace isn't lit.

as any parent of an athletically inclined child knows, every season culminates with the mixed blessing of a new trophy. Ben Turshen, an avid ice hockey player, saw the mantel in his bedroom as a ready display place for his awards. His parents backed them up in a game-opening, national anthem kind of way with a painting Ben made at age seven for a kids' art contest called "I Can Do That," sponsored by *Spy* magazine. "This is Ben's Jasper Johns," his father says.

the delft tile fireplace surround in a farmhouse built by early Dutch settlers inspired the overmantel effect, *opposite*. Veronica Krieger concocted a pyramid of porcelain after ferreting out antiques to complement the tiles. Using the large platter as a center point, she hung plates with regard to balancing their pattern and scale. The pearly gray-blue of the wall is drawn from the ground color of the tiles. Old pewter and porcelain teapots and coffeepots add dimension. The andirons are silhouettes of George Washington.

randy Ridliss had an 18th-century answer to the eyesore posed by the modernized red brick fireplace in the apartment he bought because of its quiet park-oriented view. He built out the wall, boxing in the dated 1960s hearth and restoring order to the surface as a clean plane awaiting embellishment. He painted it neoclassical yellow, applied pilasters and a bolection mantel which he picked out in white, and had a decorative mirror made by a framer. All add depth without protruding greatly into the diminutive living room.

Jeanne Taylor opted to call attention to this short, cut-corner wall with its square cutout fireplace. "I think of the surface as a picture," she says. The designer went wall-to-wall with glazed tile, trying to play out the Aegean blues and whites that resonated in her mind after a trip to Greece. Figurative tiles are bordered around the firebox and worked into the scheme to create a "painting," precluding the need for a mantel. This is chimneypiece as mood-setter for dining.

p aint-grade lumber and a cabinetmaker were the only requisites for re-creating a mantel respectful of an old house that had had its classical detailing renovated away, *top*. "It was *very* affordable," says designer Lynn Peterson. Understated adornment is supplied by an antique oval mirror and a still life of finials and banister balls. Their peeling finishes establish a soft transition from the crisp white mantel to the tea-stained wall hue.

a mantel acts as an interim showcase for assorted bric-a-brac, *above*. Until Doug Turshen tracked down an appropriate piece to hang over a fireplace, he warehoused his "pairs" collection here. Related only by scale and a certain decorousness, the cut-glass, porcelain, and wood ornaments form an unexpected mantelscape.

repetition is its own reward. On a plain wood chimneypiece rubbed with beeswax,
a series of shell prints and jugs—none of them old or particularly valuable—bring out
the best in each other simply through association. Grouping things for balance and
varying the shape, size, and shade gets the job done. Birds' nests and robins' eggs intermix.
The reiteration of round forms gives the prints and assorted objects common ground.

One method of toning down an unwanted stone hearth is to paint it. That's what Kristiina Ratia did in a narrow room where the masonry felt too heavy for the space. The subtlety of whitewashed stone throws a beguilingly simple setup into relief: A pair of candlestick lamps add the warmth of incandescent lighting (wiring is tacked along the crease of the wood mantel) and an old framed document is hung with a laurel wreath made by Kristiina.

an antique mantel was reused by architect John Milner in the 18th-century-style home of Suzanne and Ralph Roberts, *above*. The candle niche carved out of the plaster wall, cooking tools, and serving vessels evoke a rural colonial ambience.

irreverance is a virtue in the hands of Judyth van Amringe. Given free rein to decorate a guesthouse, she stenciled the living room, *opposite,* with tumbling type and lines of poetry. She cloned the mantel, using brackets to support a shelf of like proportion above, then painted doodles in circus colors over every inch of both. The owner's antique toy collection is displayed on the twin mantels and on a blanket chest.

Photographer and former stylist Anita Calero is driven to create still lifes wherever she goes—a professional hazard. Her mantel presents a long, narrow platform for one of her most appealing arrangements, *left*. She stages and balances crayon-color objects of similar scale the way a child builds with blocks. Painted cubes mix with dice, glass vessels, and her collection of 1920s pottery by Berndt Friberg. An old garden table and a miniature ladder call out the reds.

Traditional needn't mean predictable. Don Black marched a seemingly unaffiliated group of items—Chinese exportware, an ostrich egg, a thimble-shaped brass sewing kit, a carved angel from a Viennese church, and a candlestick—across his Federal-style marble mantel, *right*. He hung an 18th-century English portrait as foundation. The fire surround, snagged at auction in California, is a fine one.

ʄind something you like and make it significant by collecting it," advises Tom
Grotta. He and his wife, Rhonda Brown, live that philosophy. Their house is their
gallery; the fine crafts they sell are their passion. Silhouetting the pristine shapes
of Bob Stocksdale's turned-wood bowls across the mantel at once highlights their
individual beauty and identifies them as a body of work by one artist, *above*.
Ditto for the collages hung over them, a series of studies for weavings by Helena
Hernmarck. The horizontality streamlines the old mantel.

ſanford Smith and Patricia Lynch Smith are collectors and dealers in folk art.
Their hearth is a backdrop for a quirky combination of contemporary and
antique work, *right:* Michael di Pasquale's pottery vase, a 19th-century lead and
copper weather vane, Helen Codero's clay "Storyteller Doll," a contemporary
Native American fire screen, and a couple gopher garden figurines. Clay-colored
walls enrich the mix and call attention to the simplicity of the white mantel.

there's an upstairs-downstairs sensibility about the commingling of an Adam-style chimneypiece with yellowware crockery, but a one-note palette seems to make it all hang together, *opposite.* Kristiina Ratia found the mantel in an antique shop and let it dictate the hue of the surroundings in a room too small to absorb an array of color. The walls are sponge-painted, affording some tonal variation. A mirror helps open up the space.

that his turn-of-the-century Beaux Arts fireplace, *above,* came complete with mirrored overmantel put Brian McCarthy ahead of the game, decoratively speaking. The quest then was for curios appropriate to the setting. He came across a 19th-century French Empire clock, made from a cannonball, with a sunburst face—desirable not just for its rarity but also for its dimensionality and its finished back. He framed it with a pair of gilt bronze candlesticks and hydrangeas in mossy pots, the latter to dilute the formality of the antiques.

roger de Cabrol found a gouache-and-pencil drawing of the Pont Neuf by Christo a perfect fit for the overmantel here, and he placed a carved African head in front of it. His elegant screen, with detailing in bronze, is designed to call out the clean geometry of the square firebox. The designer's studied, spare scheme represents a purposefully contemporary treatment of period architecture in a designer showhouse. The symmetrical layout of the furnishings, all of his design, is pure 18th century; their stark lines, very today.

- **Hunt up an old** curb fender in an antique shop or have one fabricated as a fireplace surround. It's a nostalgic warming seat or place to dry wet gloves and hats.

- **Have a trio of** mirrors installed as an overmantel. Trim between and around them with stock molding.

- **Line up a bottle** collection across a mantel. Pour water in some, stand a single flower in a few, tint the water with a drop of food dye in some, leave others empty.

- **Load a mantel** with all-of-a-kind china: bowls, teacups, plates on stands. Leave space at either end for tall candelabra.

- **Hang a still life** painting over a mantel and re-create the still life on the mantel.

- **Arrange pairs of** vases symmetrically across a mantel and fill all of them with the same kind of flower.

- **Place a metal** tray of stack candles of different heights inside the fireplace and light them instead of logs.

- **Lean a large** framed black-and-white photograph on a bare mantel to make a strong, stark statement.

- **Face a chimney-** piece with mirror to intensify the fire glow.

- **Box in the** overmantel area (use wood cut to the same depth as the mantel-piece) to create a Bauhaus-like, shadow box effect, framing whatever you place inside it.

- **Hang decorative** plates or medallions within the carved panels on the front of the chimneypiece.

- **Stand an iron** grate or other metal artifact in front of the firebox instead of a conventional screen.

- **Put a large glass** bottle filled with water inside the fireplace and light a stack candle behind it. The water will magnify the moving flame.

- **Tack a textile** border, a length of scalloped crochet work, or a band of lace around the edges of the mantel.

bed

A bed generally presides over the room

in which it stands, so its appearance is critical.

Changing the bed can change the bedroom,

and that can be as easy, and as inexpensive, as

outfitting it with new linens. Beds can be

romantic or tailored, extravagant or austere,

layered or nearly naked. You can buy one

off the rack or have every bit of it custom made,

right down to the box spring. Futons,

trundle beds, sleigh beds, and daybeds make it

possible to camouflage the bed in a room

of multiple use. No matter where it's

placed or how it's dressed, a good bed must

be warm, comfortable, and seductive.

Peter Frank's bedroom seems to scream with quiet. And not just because of its palette of creamy neutrals. Soft surfaces and lack of pattern invoke a sense of calm. Attention is given to detailing but not in the expected ways; no designer linens or custom bedcover here. A nearly naked bed is laid with a wool blanket, a coverless duvet, and muslin pillowcases. But considered touches, like a well-padded cotton-upholstered headboard, wall-mounted swing-arm lamps, and an art rail (made of lumberyard molding) that creates a gallery wall bestow an all-at-arm's-length luxury upon simple fittings.

it takes only a few been-around-the-block tag-sale finds to build a little character in an extra bedroom. Ingrid Leess's stripped-pine chest, *above,* does double duty as dresser and night table. Bed linens and table runner, plus a sparsely patterned white wallpaper, crisply set off the patina of the old bed, makeup mirror, and chest.

a Directoire headboard, an 18th-century French Régence chair, a 19th-century English gilt-bronze mirror, pillows stacked Russian-style, a 1930s American neck roll, and a new cotton bedspread from Pottery Barn would seem to make strange bedfellows, *opposite.* But Brian McCarthy pulls them together with aplomb and throws in some eastern influence in the carpet and a framed study for a chinoiserie mural he commissioned for one of his clients. Subtlety in coloration and clarity of line and purpose combine to make it work.

twin beds are a versatile guest room solution, allowing the space to be shared by those who don't necessarily wish to share a bed, *below.* William Diamond and Anthony Baratta, working in a limited space, closely positioned the beds and eliminated the need for night tables. The designers framed out the wall behind the bed so they could cut in a niche just deep enough for books. Benches at the foot of each bed provide an extra surface for setting things down.

Joan Vass imagined a bed like a divan and had it custom made, *opposite.* A voracious reader, she envisioned a headboard high and cushy enough to lean against with a book propped up in her lap and a substantial upholstered base to balance the look. Woven stripes wrap around its curves, striking a Turkish note. A vertical leafy pattern coordinates the well-padded headboard. Antique shams vary the texture of the all-white linens.

Jennifer Houser floated the wicker bed in her master bedroom, *above,* all the better to enjoy the fireplace from center stage. She stacked table on table at bedside to accommodate her collected Edwardian silver containers, while still offering space for practical use. Pillows are layered for reading.

White feels cloudlike for a spare bedroom, with the potential to create a dreamy void that invites guests to make of it what they will, reasons Donna Gorman. Hers, *opposite,* is deliberately lean: a bed with a painted curved plywood headboard bolted to a standard metal frame, a repainted school chair, and a gooseneck standing lamp. Shelves for clothing storage are plentiful but closeted out of sight. Italian batiste sheets are luxuriously soft yet make a strong statement in a color vacuum.

donna Gorman turned a structural problem into a solution, *above.* To gain depth for bathroom storage cabinets, she had them built out through the wall into the bedroom, then veneered the protrusion and turned it into a headboard. A matching platform and built-in floating bedside tables define the unit as furniture. The box spring is made slim to keep the bed low and avoid the in-your-face impact of most king-size mattresses.

nothing brings an assortment of furnishings together faster than color. Carol Nelson's method is simple: pick a color family and stick with it. In a guest room, *left,* greens do the job of unifying old and new fittings with farmhouse architecture. Quirky accessories preclude monotony.

remember the bedroom suites of your childhood? They were gender-coded, and the gewgaws matched—antiqued white with curlicue hardware for girls, caramel colored and knobby for boys. Christopher Coleman hauled his old paired dressers into the city, had them parchment-finished, and attached luggagelike handles with latch details. They frame his bed, replacing night tables. Small stools hold a telephone, a book, or a glass of water.

a bed can feel like a small boat on a calm sea. That's what Maggy Fellman had in mind when she designed a shipshape bedroom: "I wanted it to have the least amount of stuff I could get away with." So she fabricated a bed by arranging storage units in a U, having a platform made to lay across them, and topping it with a firm foam mattress. Collected quilts, which rotate as bedcovers, and clothing are stowed in bins and drawers; luggage fills the cavity under the platform, in the center. Wall-mounted bedside shelves and swivel lamps keep the floor furniture-free.

Minimal and monastic are words that spring to mind to describe Anita Calero's bed, *right*. The headboard is a modern classic by George Nakashimaya; the table, a 1935 design by Joseph Aronson. The blankets and crucifix are bits of nostalgia ferried along into adult life from her childhood. Stacked pillows soften the austerity of the angular furniture.

Carlos Mota's bedroom has its highs and lows, *left*. The box spring sits on the floor, nicely camouflaged by an upholstered wooden surround. A three-legged table, made from a piece of marble and the base of a stool, lines up with the mattress height. A shapely modern vase and lily stand tall.

$a$ntique pocket watches are beautiful, but few of us carry them around. Carole Manchester hung one on her upholstered headboard in harmony with her vintage linens and in lieu of a conventional clock. It's suspended from an antique stickpin that's jabbed into the batting through a woven ribbon, which is tied off in a floppy bow to serve as a visual anchor.

a floating headboard unit centers a queen-size bed and acts as bridge between the master bedroom and a dressing room. Architect James Biber designed the piece using the imagery of stacked suitcases. He alternated beech and anigre woods to call out the sections. On the dressing room side, drawers open to an ample 2-foot depth. On the sleeping side, smaller drawers are pullouts lined with felt, so keys, change, and jewelry can be dropped inaudibly. The telephone and clock are wired through the unit to floor sockets. The architect broke through the wall to a smaller, adjacent bedroom to create the dressing room, seen through open French doors, where he teamed up old oak office chairs with a table of his design.

When sheet designer Anki Spets couldn't find a bed she liked, she invented one, *opposite*. The aluminum bed on casters, fabricated from commercial scaffold fittings, is now sold through her company, Area. Her own bed, the prototype, is proportioned for the kind of mattress with sleeping pad she grew up with in Sweden, made by Dux. The stretch terry-cloth fitted sheets are also by Dux. Striped pillowcases and duvet covers are in a random mix of Anki's woven linen designs, inspired by old Scandinavian ticking.

bold color, strong line, and un-bedroom furniture push the boundaries in bedroom decor, *above*. Mark McDonald revisits the middle years of the 20th century in furnishing his, as he does elsewhere in his apartment. A graphic Dutch blanket commands attention. Opaque floor-to-ceiling vermilion velvet drapes and an ebony enameled chest by Norman Bel Geddes reinforce a spirited scheme. The floor lamp is a rare one by Buffet. Black linens make this a turn-back-and-slip-in sleeping arrangement.

In their guest house, designer Kerstin and author Sten Enbom were moved, in the spirit of the old Scandinavian cupboard bed, to build in a pair of curtained daybeds that flank the doorway. Kerstin's handwork is evidenced in the assortment of stenciled and trimmed pillows; Sten's, in the woodwork of the bed and a shelf just deep enough for bedside reading. A serene Gustavian palette and thoughtful detailing qualify this as a sitting room as well as a sleeping place.

- **Get a bargain on** an old headboard because it's lacking its runners and footboard. Wedge it between your bed and the wall to stabilize it.

- **Lay an area rug** over the blanket in lieu of a bedspread. Choose a hooked, kilim, rya, or flokati smaller than the mattress surface so the blanket frames it in a complementary color.

- **Give up floor** space to simplify your bedroom and make the bed an island of calm. Enlarge a closet and outfit it to store all your clothing (plus dressers and shoe racks), creating less-is-more surroundings for sleep.

- **Hang mosquito** netting from a central point above the bed. Open the windows and unfurl the gauzy netting in warm weather. Tie it overhead in a plump knot during the day.

- **Stand a piece of** furniture—a chaise, a bench, a trunk, or even a stack of antique luggage— at the foot of a bed where space is ample. The dividend: a place to drop clothes or bedspread.

- **Make a long** neck roll about 10 inches in diameter to run the full width of the bed, as the French do. Place it at the head and lean pillows against it.

- **Leave the frame** of a canopy bed of any vintage uncurtained, to give it a contemporary makeover.

- **Let a desk or** dressing table double as a night table in a room where space is tight.

- **Construct a** triangular solid, with the long side equal to the mattress width, that stands 10 inches higher than the mattress height. Position your bed in a corner and use the triangular form as a headboard/night table combo to back it up.

- **Use a rectangular** coffee table, run lengthwise, as a generous bedside table for a twin bed.

directory

DESIGNERS

Aparicio, Carlos
Carlos Aparicio Associates
30 E. 67th Street
New York, NY 10021
(212) 794-3642

Baratta, Anthony
Diamond Baratta Designs
270 Lafayette Street
New York, NY 10012
(212) 966-8892

Barsanti, Daniel
Healing Barsanti
243 E. 60th Street
New York, NY 10022
(212) 753-0222

Bierman, Bruce
Bruce Bierman Design
29 W. 15th Street
New York, NY 10011
(212) 243-1935

Black, Don
156 E. 37th Street
New York, NY 10016
(212) 684-7198

Coleman, Christopher
Christopher Coleman Design
250 W. 54th Street
New York, NY 10019
(212) 616-8663

de Cabrol, Roger
Roger de Cabrol Interior
    Design Inc.
121 E. 24th Street
New York, NY 10010
(212) 353-2827

Diamond, William
Diamond Baratta Designs
270 Lafayette Street
New York, NY 10012
(212) 966-8892

Donnenfeld, Marc
Artifice Inc.
140 Nassau Street
New York, NY 10038
(212) 267-1690

Enbom Kerstin
Immersby
01150 Söderkulla, Finland
(358-9) 877-9941

Foley, Tricia
1388 Lexingon Avenue
New York, NY 10128
(212) 348-0074

Foster, Michael
Michael Foster Design
250 W. 57th Street
New York, NY 10107
(212) 957-0809

Gorman, Donna
Donna Gorman, Inc.
1115 Weed Street
New Canaan, CT 06840
(203) 972-3685

Hagan, Victoria
Victoria Hagan Interiors
654 Madison Avenue
New York, NY 10021
(212) 888-1178

Healing, Patricia
Healing Barsanti
243 E. 60th Street
New York, NY 10022
(212) 753-0222

Houser, Jennifer
Table Art by Jennifer Houser
PO Box 642
Sag Harbor, NY 11963
(516) 537-5532

Lee, Richard
220 Park Avenue South
New York, NY 10003
(212) 254-7175

Leess, Ingrid
228 Canoe Hill Road
New Canaan, CT 06840
(203) 972-0631

Letelier, Jorge
Letelier-Rock Design Inc.
1020 Madison Avenue
New York, NY 10021
(212) 988-2398

McCarthy, Brian
Brian J. McCarthy Inc.
1414 6th Avenue
New York, NY 10019
(212) 308-7600

Peterson, Lynn
Motif Designs
20 Jones Street
New Rochelle, NY 10802
(914) 633-1170

Ratcliff, Susan
Susan Ratcliff Design
5 E. 82nd Street
New York, NY 10028
(212) 794-3462

Ratia, Kristiina
Kristiina Ratia Design Inc.
PO Box 997
Norwalk, CT 06820
(203) 852-0027

Ridliss, Randy
37 Gramercy Park East
New York, NY 10011
(212) 982-3061

Riley, Charles
Charles Riley
245 8th Avenue
New York, NY 10011
(212) 647-9128

Rock, Sheryl
Letelier-Rock Design Inc.
1020 Madison Avenue
New York, NY 10021
(212) 988-2398

Taylor, Jeanne
Jeanne Taylor Interiors
521 Riversville Road
Greenwich, CT 06831
(203) 622-0750

Train, Betsy
Betsy McCue Train Design
344 Club View Drive
Great Falls, VA 22066
(703) 759-1595

van Amringe, Judyth
97 Williams Street
Providence, RI 02906
(401) 861-8056

van Vliet, Geertruda
160 Florida Hill Road
Greenwich, CT 06877
(203) 431-9395

ARCHITECTS

Biber, James
Pentagram
204 5th Avenue
New York, NY 10010
(212) 683-7071

de Polo, Harry
de Polo + Nelson Architecture
PO Box 68
West Cornwall, CT 06796
(860) 672-3333

Nelson, Carol
de Polo + Nelson Architecture
PO Box 68
West Cornwall, CT 06796
(860) 672-3333

GALLERIES

Brown/Grotta Gallery
39 Grumman Hill Road
Wilton, CT 06897
(203) 834-0623

Gansevoort Gallery
72 Gansevoort Street
New York, NY 10014
(212) 633-0555

Smith Gallery
PO Box 20385
New York, NY 10011
(212) 744-6171

index